The Leavening of Life

The Leavening of Life

Contemporary hymns for different times & seasons

Pat Bennett

wild goose publications www.ionabooks.com

Copyright © 2021 Pat Bennett

Published 2021 by
Wild Goose Publications
Suite 9, Fairfield,
1048 Govan Road, Glasgow G51 4XS, Scotland
www.ionabooks.com
Wild Goose Publications is the publishing division of the Iona Community.
Scottish Charity No. SC003794. Limited Company Reg. No. SC096243.

ISBN 978-1-84952-749-1

The publishers gratefully acknowledge the support of the Drummond Trust,
3 Pitt Terrace, Stirling FK8 2EY in producing this book.

Cover image © Fabiobalbi | Dreamstime.com

All rights reserved. Apart from the circumstances described below relating to non-commercial use, no part of this publication may be reproduced in any form or by any means, including photocopying or any information storage or retrieval system, without written permission from the publisher via PLSclear.com.

Non-commercial use: The material in this book may be used non-commercially for worship and group work without written permission from the publisher. If photocopies of sections are made, please make full acknowledgement of the source, and report usage to CLA or other copyright organisation.

Pat Bennett has asserted her right in accordance with the Copyright, Designs and Patents Act, 1988, to be identified as the author of this work.

Overseas distribution:
Australia: Willow Connection Pty Ltd, Unit 4A, 3-9 Kenneth Road,
Manly Vale, NSW 2093
New Zealand: Pleroma, Higginson Street, Otane 4170, Central Hawkes Bay

Printed by Bell & Bain, Thornliebank, Glasgow

Contents

Acknowledgements   7

Introduction   9

Celebration, commitment and response   11

Bread   12

Gifts   15

Love   18

Celebration   19

Commitment   21

Affirmation   22

Offering   23

Pathways   24

Speech   26

Stories   27

God's place   28

The Way   30

Struggle, separation and silence   31

Yearnings   32

Creator God   34

Psalm 23   36

Psalm 116   37

In this darkness   38

Remembrance   40

Farewells   43

Psalm 130   44

The Leavening of Life

Where?   45

Questions   46

Marking the seasons   47

Advent and Christmas   49

Watching   51

Telling   52

Longing   54

Incarnation   56

Angels' song   58

Iona carol   61

Holy Week and Easter   63

Easter windows   65

Encounter   67

The last journey   68

Easter story   70

Christ is here!   72

Lord of Life and Resurrection   74

Sources   77

Acknowledgements

I am grateful to my colleague John L. Bell for writing the tunes 'Bridge of waiting', 'Gillamoor' and 'Firth of Kelvin' for the texts In this darkness, Longing and Gifts, for permission to use the tunes 'Nafziger' and 'Laying down' for the texts Bread and Remembrance, and for providing the harmonisation for the tune 'Another place'.

I am likewise grateful to Stephen Fischbacher of Fischy Music for permission to use his variation on the tune 'Madrid' for the texts Angels' song and Christ is here!.

Introduction

*'[The Kingdom of God] is like yeast
that a woman took and mixed in
with three measures of flour
until all of it was leavened.'*

Luke 13:20–21

*'Through all these elemental things
your leavening power unleash:
transform the textures of my life –
the dough becoming flesh.'*

From Bread

Hymns have always been a significant part of my life: as a child I loved singing them and was captivated by the poetry and cadences of certain lines long before I understood their meaning. Later they would become one of the ways through which my own understandings about the Incarnation and its implications evolved – indeed I suspect most of us can trace a changing thread of hymns and songs that accompanies our pilgrimage of faith, some of which we might now struggle to sing. More recently, using the discipline of hymnodic form myself has been a fruitful way of exploring different dimensions of life, and of the way these can be transformed by the leaven of the Kingdom of which Jesus speaks.

In all of this, my experiences have simply echoed the larger story of the role of hymns from the early church onwards. As we know from Acts (16:25), Ephesians (5:19) and Colossians (3:16) hymn-singing was a routine part of the personal and communal life of the early Christians. Some hymns were clearly used for praising God – Pliny the Younger, writing to the emperor Trajan around AD 112, describes Christians singing 'antiphonal hymns to Christ' – but others allowed early Christians to articulate their growing understanding of the significance of the life, death and resurrection of Jesus. We can see this clearly in the fragments of early Christological hymns in the Epistles (Philippians 2:6–11, Colossians 1:15–20, 1 Timothy 3:16) which are both economical in form but also thick and rich articulations of a profound mystery. As with all good texts, these early hymns do not spell out detailed answers but instead offer finger-and-toe-holds for getting traction on an idea, spaces for questions to be asked, and further depths to explore on return visits.

The hymns in this book reflect different aspects of my own ongoing engagement with this ancient tool for exploration and expression. Some were written as responses to stories in the Gospels or for particular services in the liturgical cycle; some represent deliberate explorations of perennial Christian themes such as love and commitment; others have a different biographical trajectory beginning in specific events; where relevant I have shared some of these details alongside the texts. The resulting collection neither is, nor aspires to be, comprehensive in its themes or definitive in its theology.

Pat Bennett
Scotland
January 2021

Celebration, commitment and response

Bread

As once you served a waiting crowd
when someone shared their bread,
so still, through freely offered life,
your hungry world is fed.

For, having planted seed corn deep
in every human heart,
there, quickened by affirming grace,
your Kingdom's work can start.

I open to your ripening power
the pattern of my days:
the salty sweat of daily work,
my rest and leisure's ways.

I offer to your shaping hands
the stories of my life:
the hopeful lines of joy and faith,
the darker words of strife.

Through all these elemental things
your leavening power unleash:
transform the textures of my life –
the dough becoming flesh.

Then break me with the hands of grace,
that living I may prove
a generous bread of Kingdom life –
of healing, peace and love.

Text © Pat Bennett
Tune: 'Nafziger'
Music John L. Bell, copyright © 2000, 2002 WGRG, Iona Community, Glasgow, Scotland www.wildgoose.scot

This hymn was written during a week on Iona in which guests reflected on, wrote about and made bread together. During the breadmaking I was particularly struck by the change in the texture of the dough as I worked and kneaded it –

how it began to feel much more like a living thing. I was also caught by a remark made by the baker leading the week about how the dough takes up salt from the traces of sweat in the hands working it. The move to then thinking about the life of faith through the story of bread – its making and sharing – seemed a very natural one.

This text works well as a communion hymn but would also be suitable for commitment services.

Celebration, commitment and response 15

Gifts

The Leavening of Life

As we tread out the paths of our lives,
other trav'llers we meet as we go
bring us glimpses and whispers and signs
of rich worlds that we do not yet know.
As we savour these gifts of the way
may they nourish our lives so that we
find the courage and hope to go on
to the places God calls us to be.

As we read in the texts of our faith
words long loved, and the ones we deplore,
we find waymarks and pointers towards
deeper patterns we've yet to explore.
As we search out these gifts of the word
may they nurture our lives so that we
grow in wisdom, in peace and in love
as the signs that God asks us to be.

As we come to your table O God,
drawn inside by Love's urgent appeal,
we find bread to give strength for the road;
we find wine to refresh and to heal.
As we share in these gifts of your grace,
come and meet us in them, so that we
through encounter might find ourselves changed
into people you long us to be.

Text: © Pat Bennett
Tune: 'Firth of Kelvin'
Music John L. Bell, copyright © 2021 WGRG, Iona Community, Glasgow, Scotland
www.wildgoose.scot

Verse 3 could be omitted for a non-communion service.

Love

For Ellie and James

Here as we gather, greeting this day's gladness,
we call to mind the love that sets us free:
faithfully sharing all our joy and sadness,
God's love reveals how love is meant to be.

So may love shape and shine through all our living,
temper our actions, fill and warm our speech,
make us in all things patient and forgiving –
kindness and caring always in our reach.

In all decisions may love guide our choices,
show us the way to peace instead of strife,
help us to silence selfish, grudging voices,
lead us to live a generous open life.

Then through the years may love grow ever brighter,
nurture and keep us, always guide us home,
heighten each joy, make every burden lighter –
wellspring of grace, where hope and strength are known.

Text: © Pat Bennett
Tune: 'Lord of the years' (11 10 11 10)

This text – based on the famous passage in I Corinthians 13 – was written for the wedding of young friends but would be suitable for other occasions too.

Celebration

Refrain: Sing high praises to God,
the source of all life and all loving;
rock upon which we stand,
vision that calls us on.

This is the calling of God
to all who will hear and embrace it:
'Leave safety and self behind
and follow where I lead.'
Sing high praises to God ...

So we give thanks on this day
for those who, fearing but faithful,
answered that summons and came
bringing God's life to this place.
Sing high praises to God ...

This is the purpose of God
for all who will answer his calling –
that they build a Kingdom shaped
by justice, peace and love.
Sing high praises to God ...

So we give thanks on this day
for those whose speaking and actions
make of this place a house
where God's love is known.
Sing high praises to God ...

This is the vision of God
and all who are holding his purpose –
that one day his Kingdom's love
will heal all life on earth.
Sing high praises to God ...

So on this day, in this place,
we pledge ourselves to that vision,
off'ring our lives and our love
to serve the Kingdom's call.
Sing high praises to God …

Text: © Pat Bennett
Tune: 'Salva feste dies' (irregular)

This hymn was commissioned by St Luke's Episcopal Church, Minneapolis, for their Centenary Founders' Day celebration in Autumn 2014. While particularly suited to services of celebration/dedication/commissioning, etc., it need not be limited to these.

Commitment

God-in-Community, within your word we see
the waymarks for this path that we are taking:
living without conceal, caring for common weal,
and forging bonds to hold when all is breaking.

Through cords that free and bind, in common life we find
the tools to do this task that we are sharing:
wisdom to know the right, courage for facing might,
and words to tell of hope beyond despairing.

So we together stand, offering heart and hand
committed to this journey of relation.
And as we take our place, gift us the holy grace
to love and live set free from calculation.

Text: © Pat Bennett
Tune: 'Down Ampney' (66 11 D)

This hymn was written for the Iona Community's annual hallowing service on Iona, at which new members are received into the Community and existing members renew their commitment. The final phrase is based on a line in one of George MacLeod's prayers: 'too often we have made your church an institution/when you want it to be a chaos of uncalculating love'.

Although written for a very specific occasion, it would be suitable for other services of commitment, especially in a community context.

Affirmation

God beyond knowledge, yet close to us here,
our touchstone, our lodestar, in faith and in fear;
your presence we know in the dark before dawn
as courage is kindled and hope is reborn.

God without limits, yet sharing our flesh,
you speak for the silenced, release the oppressed
and call us to follow, in all things to prove –
the tools of your Spirit, the signs of your love.

Lord to your purpose our living we pledge:
to go beyond comfort and stand at life's edge,
to love and to live without safety, and so
to shape and inhabit your Kingdom of hope.

Text: © Pat Bennett
Tune: 'Slane' (10 11 11 11)

This hymn is based on an affirmation in the Iona Abbey Worship Book *written by Iona Community members Jan Sutch Pickard and Brian Woodcock following their arrest at Faslane Naval base during a protest against nuclear weapons. It is particularly suitable for, but not limited to, services of dedication/commitment.*

Celebration, commitment and response 23

Offering

My feet for God's pathways, wherever they wend;
my hands for God's purpose, to build and to tend;
my voice for God's love and God's justice to speak;
my life for God's Kingdom, whose coming I seek.

Text: © Pat Bennett
Tune: 'Columcille' (11 11 11 11)

This text was written for a recommitment liturgy for associate members of the Iona Community. It would work well as part of an act of commitment and also as a short song during a symbolic action.

Pathways

Lord, your life revealed the wholeness
at the heart of God's design,
as with love and deep compassion
you embraced this world through time.
So may we, who as your body
seek to do the work of God,
find and follow paths of healing
which your human feet once trod.

As you comforted the suffering –
those who touched you, called your name –
there your listening and your speaking
heard and answered cries of pain.
So may we, who try to follow
on this pathway you have shown,
build a place of quiet sharing
where no-one need weep alone.

When you brought home lost and leper
God's intent was there made plain.
Through unlocking shuttered ears and eyes
you revealed his will again.
So may we, who try to follow
on this pathway you have shown,
bring God's purpose and his patterns
where their beauties are unknown.

In the fullness of your loving
we can sense God's close embrace,
as by strong and generous living
you make clear his care and grace.
So may we, who try to follow
on these pathways you have shown,
of your body make a healing place
where God's wholeness can be known.

Text: © Pat Bennett
Tune: 'Beach Spring' (87 87 D)

Written for a Diocesan Healing Day, this text is a reflection on the different elements which were part of the healing ministry of Jesus, in which we are all called to participate.

Although the text works well with 'Beach Spring', the shape of some lines means it will not automatically work with all tunes of 87 87 D metre. 'Holy Manna', 'Lewis folk melody', 'Nettleton' and 'Transformation' are other possibilities.

Speech

For Mike

O God, your words split silence wide
calling forth from darkness – light!
Your voice went out across the void
and tamed the chaos with its might.
Your song gave life to all the world,
gave form and voice to all and each;
and, breathing through the clay you had made,
gave humankind the gift of speech.

O Christ, your words split noise apart
making a quiet and sacred space.
Your voice went out across the land –
and called the wandering human race.
Your song gave life to all who heard
through struggle, turmoil, doubt or pain:
For as you spoke of hope, joy and peace
the voice of God was heard again.

So take my voice, and as I speak,
breathe your Spirit through that speech,
that every word might hold the power
to open out your Kingdom's reach:
so may my words wherever spent
in church or home or open space,
send out the voice of God once more –
the song of life, of love and grace.

Text: © Pat Bennett
Tune: 'Jerusalem' (88 88 D or DLM)

This hymn was written for the licensing of a friend as a local Methodist preacher and uses his favourite hymn tune. It is particularly suitable for services of commissioning or commitment but works well in other contexts too.

Stories

God, eternal and unchanging,
though unbound by time or place,
yet with constant, tender yearning
you sustain our human race.
History in all its colours,
present moment where we stand,
hidden future, still to open –
all are gathered in your hand.

God, who sees all human stories,
you in each your touch display;
sometimes known and sometimes hidden
you have met us on our way.
Though we may have failed or faltered,
doubted love, resisted grace,
yet, persistent, you walked with us
guiding us towards your place.

God, whose life pervades each moment,
meet us in this present hour,
as we open thought and action
to your life's transforming power.
Startle, challenge and confront us,
touch our hearts and free our hands –
so that we may see and serve you,
yield to all your love demands.

God, who stands beyond the future,
what's to come is still unknown;
yet, unchanging, you are with us
and we will not walk alone.
Go with us through doubt and darkness,
stand with us in hopeful place,
'til the chain of time is broken
and we see you face to face.

Text: © Pat Bennett
Tune: 'Blaenwern' (87 87 D)

This hymn was originally written for a Millennium service. The use of the adjective 'unchanging' in connection with God can be problematic but here it refers to God's constancy of love towards us.

God's place

O God beyond all boundaries,
you cannot be confined
by Age or moment, form or shape,
by word or creed defined.
And yet you once in human flesh
took root in time and space –
break through the fabric of our lives
and meet us in our place.

Lead us into the inner place
where we may see and own
the things that fetter and distort,
that break our spirit down.
And as we face the dark within,
so gift us with your grace,
that in the place of death we find
our resurrection place.

Go with us to the public place
to sound your *kairos* hour,
to overthrow injustices
and break oppression's power.
Then take us to the place outside
to stand with those alone,
and by our actions and our words
to make our lives their home.

So meet us in that place of hope
where heaven and earth unite,
where doubt and darkness, hate and fear
are scattered by your light.
Then by your life and power transformed
we will reveal your face
and everything we do and are
will always be your place.

Text: © Pat Bennett
Tune: 'Kingsfold' (DCM)

This hymn was written during an Easter retreat on Iona in response to exploring the Passion stories through the lens of 'place'. Life for most of us is a series of many deaths and resurrections and I have always found the idea of the graveyard as a place of new beginnings a powerful one in helping me navigate times of ending.

The Way

If you want to enter my Kingdom –
seek the place that I have shown!
For in hearts that think first of others
God desires to make his home.
When you act in quiet service –
this is where God's grace will be known.

If you want to live in my Kingdom –
spend yourselves as I have shown!
For in hearts without calculation
God is pleased to make his home.
When you give your life for others –
this is where God's love will be known.

If you want to build my Kingdom –
then be one as I have shown!
For where hearts in love are united
God delights to make his home.
When you breach a wall that separates –
this is where God's joy will be known.

All who want to share in my Kingdom –
do God's will as I have shown!
And my Father's heart will embrace you –
we will make your life our home:
As we walk the way together
you will know, as you are known.

Text: © Pat Bennett
Tune: 'Picardy' (87 87 87)

John 14:23, in which Jesus promises those who love him that 'My Father will love them, and we will come to them and make our home with them', has been a cherished verse for many years. This hymn is an attempt to tease out what the obedience of love, which is also part of v.23, might look like, based on Jesus' words and actions in his last evening with his disciples as set out in John 13 and 14. As such the text would also work well for a Maundy Thursday service.

Struggle, separation and silence

Yearnings

We bring our yearnings, Lord,
of heart and soul and mind –
to see the patterns you inspire
restored to humankind.

We yearn to see a time
when war and conflicts cease,
when turmoil fuelled by race and creed
is overcome by peace.

We yearn to know a world
where seeds of justice flower;
where burdens made by human greed
no longer wield their power.

We yearn to find the ground
where none need stand alone,
where all are welcomed, valued, loved
and know they've reached their home.

We yearn to feel at one
with all who call your name,
to breach the walls that separate
and end division's pain.

Lord, take and use our lives,
we offer them for this –
that through our yearning and your power
earth will know heaven's bliss.

Text: © Pat Bennett
Tune: Garelochside: Kenneth G Finlay (1882-1974) © Broomhill Hyndland Church of Scotland.

During the opening session of a creative week on Iona in 1999 called 'States of Bliss and Yearning', guests were asked to name a yearning they had for the world. This hymn – the first I wrote – was a distillation of what was shared, and was sung in the Abbey at the end of the week. It would never have come to fruition but for the encouragement of Alison Adam and Graham Maule of the Wild Goose Resource Group, who were leading the programme, and whose continuing critical input over the years has been much appreciated.

Creator God

Creator God, abundant life your mark,
you once poured speech into the formless dark;
and from those words sprang forth a living spark –
your inspiration
awoke creation.

And so this world, in which we live and move,
all that we sense below, around, above,
displays the imprint of your longing love –
its revelation
throughout creation.

But yet the earth is fractured, frayed and torn,
poisoned, polluted, ravaged, scarred and worn:
its treasures plundered and its beauties scorned –
our desecration
of God's creation.

From blight and guilt, we cannot walk away:
our will and actions shape the world today;
and ours the greed, insistent on its way,
whose depredations
despoil creation.

Come Holy Spirit, challenge mind and heart!
Inspire our living so that we can start
to make those choices which may yet impart
love's liberation
to your creation.

We pledge to touch all things with holy care
until your coming Kingdom ends despair;
when all the world will witness and will share
the jubilation
of healed creation.

Text: © Pat Bennett
Tune: 'Sine nomine' (10 10 10 and Alleluia)

This hymn was written in 2001 for a competition organised by Christian Ecology Link (now 'Green Christian', https://greenchristian.org.uk) and has been regularly used at climate change services and marches.

Psalm 23

For Mike

As I take this path before me,
though I may not know its ways,
God is with me on that journey –
shepherd of its nights and days.

When I stumble on broad pastures,
drink from water, cool and strong,
God is with me in that moment –
joy and hope that shape my song.

When the road is hedged by terrors
throwing shadows cold and deep,
God is with me in that moment –
rod to comfort, staff to keep.

When companions share my laughter,
hold my hand to ward off dread,
God is with me in that moment –
oil of blessing on my head.

When I see the waiting table,
hear the words worn smooth through time,
God is with me in that moment –
gift of grace in bread and wine.

As I take this path before me,
living life while facing death,
You are with me in each moment –
close as breathing, warm as breath.

Text: © Pat Bennett
Tune: 'Servant song' (87 87)

This version of Psalm 23 was written for a friend who had been given a terminal diagnosis, and I tried to imagine what some of its well-loved phrases might mean in this situation. 'Words worn smooth through time' was a favourite line of his, from the Christmas communion liturgy 'The Feast of the Christ Child' (Pat Bennett, Wild Goose Publications).

Psalm 116

I love the Lord because he heard
and came to me in my distress;
redeemed, restored, renewed my life
and so his name I'll praise and bless.

I wandered in the darkest place;
I courted death, resisted love
until, confused and full of grief,
I cried aloud to God above.

The Lord reached out his hand to me
and touched me in my deep despair;
he wiped away my bitter tears,
released my feet from every snare.

So now in God's house will I stand
before the people of his name –
lift up my voice to honour him,
his mercy, grace and love proclaim.

My vows to you I'll thus fulfil –
this is the offering I bring:
my life henceforth shall be your own,
your people serve, your praises sing.

Text: © Pat Bennett
Tune: 'Ombersley' (LM)

In this darkness

In this darkness
I do not ask to walk by light,
but to feel the touch of your hand
and understand that sight is not seeing.

In this silence
I do not ask to hear your voice,
but to sense your Spirit breathe
and know myself a word of your speaking.

In unknowing
I do not ask for fearless space,
but for grace to comprehend
that neither you nor I are diminished.

In this death
I do not seek escape from pain,
but, embracing loss, to find
the strength to cross the bridge of waiting.

Text: © Pat Bennett
Tune: 'Bridge of waiting'
Music John L. Bell, copyright © 2005 WGRG, Iona Community, Glasgow, Scotland
www.wildgoose.scot

This hymn, based on a longer text written some years ago when I was exploring a particular loss, was set to a beautiful tune by John. A recording can be found on the Wild Goose Resource Group CD I Will Not Sing Alone (Wild Goose Publications). It is probably best sung by a choir or small group.

Remembrance

For Zam, Graham and Glenn

We gather at this margin of our world
where we are held by time – from which you've gone,
to light that threshold with our love and thanks
and sing you on.

Struggle, separation and silence   41

Your vision and commitment stirred our lives,
and challenged us to move beyond confines;
in every ripple spreading from that change
your light still shines.

We celebrate your wisdom, wit and care
and treasure every gift which memory brings;
through words and acts recalled and honoured now
your voice still sings.

And though we can no longer see your face,
though touch and sound and scent of you are gone,
we know that in God's heart, as in our own,
you will live on.

Text: © Pat Bennett
Tune: 'Laying down'
Music John L. Bell, copyright © 1989 WGRG, Iona Community, Glasgow, Scotland
www.wildgoose.scot

This text was written after the death of a friend several years ago and subsequently adapted following two more recent bereavements. It works well for a funeral or a memorial service and is very easy to personalise by changing the nouns in the opening lines of the second and third verses to reflect the person being remembered: for example, another version of this hymn used 'your courage and compassion' in verse 2 and 'your wisdom, love and joy' in verse 3. The hymn is also suitable for use at other services of remembrance such as on All Souls' Day.

If the idea of 'singing someone on' feels a little awkward, then a possible alternative for verse 1 would be:

We gather at this margin of our world
where you must take a path we don't yet know,
to light that threshold with our love and thanks
and let you go.

At funerals and memorial services it is sometimes better to use a familiar tune, and the following version of the text will work with 'Eventide' (and other, though not all, 10 10 10 10 metre tunes). It too can be adapted by changing the nouns in the opening lines of the second and third verse as outlined above; you could also substitute other words in the final lines of these verses, for example: 'Your love still nurtures us, your heart still sings', etc.

We gather at this margin of our world
where we are held by time – from which you're gone,
to light that threshold with our love and thanks,
to tell your story and to sing you on.

Your vision and commitment stirred our lives,
challenging us to move beyond confines;
in every ripple spreading from that change
your energy still runs, your light still shines.

We celebrate your wisdom, wit and care
and treasure every gift which memory brings;
through words and acts recalled and honoured now
your warmth still nurtures us, your voice still sings.

And though we can no longer see your face,
though touch and sound and scent of you are gone,
we know that in God's heart, as in our own,
held in the web of love you will live on.

Text: © Pat Bennett

Farewells

We find on life's pathway as onward it tends,
in the meeting of strangers – the birthing of friends!
Through your generous welcome we found ourselves 'home' –
embraced and companioned, no longer alone.

Your courage and vision enlarged and informed us,
your kindness sustained us, your gentleness warmed us,
your joyfulness brightened, your wisdom enlightened –
to travel beside you has blessed and transformed us.

And now we would give you into the embrace
of the wind and the sea and the song of this place;
one journey is over, another begun –
go, walk beyond stars in the heart of the Son.

Text: © Pat Bennett
Tune: 'Columcille' (11 11 11 11)

This was written for the scattering of a friend's ashes at Columba's Bay on Iona. It would be very easy to adapt this for use in a different location by changing the words 'wind' and 'sea' in the second line of the final verse to 'earth' and 'sky' or to other words which reflect the place where the ashes are being placed.

Psalm 130

Out of the darkest depths,
close to the realm of death,
I cry – and hope that you will hear
my fading, faltering breath.

Were you to watch for wrongs
I know I could not stand,
but there is kindness in your heart –
forgiveness in your hand.

So I will look with hope –
as watchers in the night –
for that first softening of the dark
that speaks of coming light.

Text: © Pat Bennett
Tune: 'Southwell' (6 6 8 6)

Where?

When sorrow shrouds and numbs my waking hours,
where can I go for comfort and relief –
but to the one who knows my empty heart
and wordlessly walks with me in my grief.

When shadows smother, trapping me in fear,
where can I turn for courage and for aid –
but to the one who in the darkest night
keeps lightless vigil and is not afraid.

When silence shuts out every loving voice,
where can I find a word to help me stand –
but from the one whose speech weaves through all life
who has my name engraved upon their hand.

When strangeness cuts me off from all I know,
where can I run so I am not alone –
but to the one whose depths I cannot sound
who offers me their heart to be my home.

Text: © Pat Bennett
Tune: 'Sursum corda' (10 10 10 10)

This hymn has its roots in Isaiah 49:15 and 16 but has also been influenced by imagery in Rilke's 'The Book of Pilgrimage'.

Questions

Though day brings neither hope nor help
and comfort's arms are cold –
a hidden thread sustains my life:
God has me in his hold.

For though I find no sheltering place
from life's relentless pains –
unseen, unheard, yet with me still,
God faithfully remains.

And in that bleakest, darkest hour
when lights no longer shine,
God feels and shares my deepest grief
and joins his tears with mine.

Though how and when are not yet known,
the questions of despair
are heard, and held, within God's heart
and will be answered there.

Text: © Pat Bennett
Tune: 'I waited patiently for God' (CM)

Marking the seasons

Advent and Christmas

Watching

Watch – though the length of night
makes courage fade and fail:
God has sent out his Word –
darkness will not prevail!
As softening sky announces dawn
Emmanuel comes – hope is reborn.

Watch – though the bleak of day
leaves spirit bruised and numb:
God has sent out his Word –
healing and peace will come!
As steadfast hearts hold on through pain
Emmanuel comes – joy flows again.

Watch – though the winter's chill
binds all with barren cold:
God has sent out his Word –
death cannot keep its hold!
As frozen earth turns quick and green
Emmanuel comes – new life is seen.

Lift up the Advent cry,
shout for the world to hear:
'God has sent out his Word –
hope, joy and life are near!'
Those watching will not wait in vain –
Emmanuel comes to bring God's reign!

Text: © Pat Bennett
Tune: 'Little Cornard' (66 66 88)

Telling

Tell of a world created by God's breath
but marred and broken, captive now to death;
tell of its people hurt and astray –
and trapped in darkness, doubt and disarray.
Then sing of hope
as deepest night
is pierced by uncreated light!

Tell of the prophets through whose fiery word
God's call to peace and justice could be heard;
and tell of those whose speaking today
unlocks the plan and pattern of his way.
Then sing of hope
for words make plain
that earth will see God's Kingdom reign!

Tell of the voice of challenge and command:
'Repent! Prepare! God's coming is at hand!'
And tell of those who hearing, turn
to find the one for whom they yearn.
Then sing of hope
where offered hearts
become the place true living starts!

Tell of a woman by encounter stirred,
whose body sheltered God's incarnate Word;
and tell of those in every time
whose lives give form and face to the Divine.
Then sing of hope
that flows from the place
where God is birthed by human grace!

Tell of a baby weak and without power
whose crying sounds the dawning *kairos* hour;
tell of his life which, changing the world,
brought in God's Kingdom – now through us unfurled.
Then sing for joy
that he who came,
is with us now and comes again!

Text: © Pat Bennett
Tune: 'Veni Emmanuel' (French 15th-century plainsong melody, LM and refrain)

This carol reflects and responds to some of the traditional themes of Advent: hope; the prophets; John the Baptist; Mary; Jesus. It can be sung either in its entirety or used incrementally, perhaps in conjunction with candle-lighting, by adding a new verse each week throughout Advent.

Longing

Searching for paths in the thickets of night –
ways threading up to the promise of light:
    longing for Dayspring's dawn,
    longing for Dayspring's dawn.

Straining to hear 'midst the babel of noise –
whispers of justice, its hope and its joys:
    longing for Wisdom's voice,
    longing for Wisdom's voice.

Aching to find through the chill of despair –
touches of warmth, the beginnings of care:
    longing for Love's embrace,
    longing for Love's embrace.

Dreaming of spring while in winter's bleak hold –
quickening life which then waits to unfold:
    longing for Stems to bud,
    longing for Stems to bud.

Bright Morning Star and a Word in the night –
Love shows its face through Emmanuel's light:
    waiting gives way to life;
    longing dissolves into joy!

Text: © Pat Bennett
Tune: 'Gillamoor'
Music John L. Bell, copyright © 2021 WGRG, Iona Community, Glasgow, Scotland
www.wildgoose.scot

This is another carol which can be used incrementally – adding a new verse each week during Advent. It was written during a difficult time and takes its inspiration from the great 'O Antiphons' – seven short verses composed in the 6th or 7th century and sung at Vespers during the last seven days of Advent. Invoking a rich mosaic of imagery from the prophecies of Isaiah ('Wisdom', 'Stem of Jesse', 'Dayspring' 'Key of David', 'Emmanuel', etc.) these ancient liturgical texts look with longing for the return of the Messiah. The 10 10 7 7 metre is not a common one but an alternative tune (which also marries very well with the feel of the text) is 'Kenosis', by Norman Warren.

Incarnation

From farthest east to utmost west,
from primal light to earth's final dawn,
let all creation sing of Christ –
the Prince who was of a virgin born.

Though uncreated and source of all,
from deepest love and compassion he
himself took on created form –
becoming flesh to set it free.

In secret smallness new life begins –
mysterious moment, not seen or heard:
an unbreached place opens up to love
as God speaks out the Incarnate Word.

And so with swiftness the Lord comes down
to Mary's body, his sheltering place;
there he whose breath does sustain all life,
is held and nurtured by a woman's grace.

In time, the babe whom the angel named,
her pain releases into the light:
Christ whom the Baptist had known with joy
while both were hidden still from human sight.

So weak and helpless he lies in straw,
his hands embracing the cradle's wood;
and though he names and feeds the birds,
he now himself depends on human food.

The planets sing as they cross the sky,
and night responds to the angels' paean;
the shepherds kneel at their Shepherd's feet
where God at last can be plainly seen!

From farthest east to utmost west,
from primal light to earth's final dawn:
Let all creation sing to Christ –
the Prince who was of a virgin born.

Text: © Pat Bennett, from a retranslation and paraphrase by Nick Swarbrick and Pat Bennett of the Latin text 'A solis ortus cardine', by Coelius Sedulius (died c. 450).

Tune: 'The Truth from above' (English traditional carol, LM)

This text began life as an informal project with a colleague exploring the language and theology of the first seven verses of a Latin acrostic poem recounting Christ's life from birth to resurrection. Wrestling with Sedulius' words and imagery enriched and deepened my own thinking about the Incarnation and I wanted to try to capture some of those ideas in the form of a carol based as directly as possible on his text.

'A solis', which was widely known in the church from late antiquity and medieval times until the end of the seventeenth century, has formed the basis of a number of hymns, including 'From lands that see the sun arise', by J.M. Neale.

Angels' song

Come, join the angels' song:
'Glory be to God on high!'
Raise voices loud and strong:
'On the earth be peace to all!'
Down through the velvet sky
God breathes a healing sigh:
heard in a baby's cry.
Shout with joy for Christ is born!

Shepherds out watching heard:
'Glory be to God on high!'
Though scared their hearts were stirred.
'On the earth be peace to all!'
Let's go and run with them
downhill to Bethlehem,
look in the manger – then
shout with joy for Christ is born!

Hearing a bright star sing:
'Glory be to God on high!'
wise ones searched for the king.
'On the earth be peace to all!'
Let's go and kneel with them,
worship in Bethlehem,
offer ourselves – and then
shout with joy for Christ is born!

Come, join the angels' song:
'Glory be to God on high!'
Lift voices loud and strong:
'On the earth be peace to all!'
God is no more concealed –
this babe his face revealed;
through him creation's healed!
Shout with joy for Christ is born!

Text: © Pat Bennett
Tune: 'Madrid' (adapted by Stephen Fischbacher ©)

The Leavening of Life

This carol – in the tradition of 'Come, children, join and sing' – was written for the 2014 Christmas Day service in Iona Abbey. Fischy Music's 12/8 version of the tune 'Madrid', with its catchy interlude, gives it a lively dancing feel – and we did indeed dance up and down the aisles in between the verses! This collection also contains an alternative set of words for use at Easter (Christ is here!, p.72). The regular version of the tune will also work with these verses but the feel will be a little more sedate.

Iona carol

Jesus is born:
formed in a womb and now a baby,
Jesus is born.
Swaddled and small, he sleeps in hay.
Setting aside his power and glory,
homeless he enters human story:
Christ comes to earth.

Jesus is born:
angels announce a joyful message,
Jesus is born.
'Peace on the earth, goodwill to all.
This is the hour God shows his favour,
sending his Son, Creation's Saviour':
Hope comes to earth.

Jesus is born:
high overhead a star is shining,
Jesus is born.
Earth houses uncreated light.
Now is the hold of darkness broken
as hearts and minds to God are opened:
Light comes to earth.

Jesus is born:
this night the world is changed for ever.
Jesus is born,
and in this babe for all to see,
Love is revealed; God's heart lies open
as the Incarnate Word is spoken:
God comes to earth.

Text: © Pat Bennett
Tune: 'The infant King' (Basque traditional, irregular)

This carol was written for the 2000 Christmas Eve service in Iona Abbey, and is included in the Church Hymnary 4th Edition *(Canterbury Press).*

Holy Week and Easter

Easter windows

As Jesus kneels and washes feet
a window opens wide –
to show a different way of life
where love displaces pride.

Then, as he breaks and shares the bread
and pours and blesses wine,
the simple actions point towards
dimensions beyond time.

Out from the upper room he goes
to face a fearful choice
where, ringing through his willing 'Yes',
we hear and know faith's voice.

Despite his dying agony
his words are full of care;
and God is glimpsed in darkened glass
as hope beyond despair.

The three-day silence of the tomb,
Christ's hiddenness from sight –
reveal a patient God, who waits
until the time is right.

But then in meetings with his friends,
through sight and touch and breath,
God's deepest mystery unfolds –
that life is born through death!

'Whoever turns and looks at me
will see the Father too;
His face is shown and clarified
through all I say and do.'

Text: © Pat Bennett
Tune: 'Nun danket all'/Gräfenberg (CM)

66   *The Leavening of Life*

This hymn was inspired by a reflection given by the Rev. Leith Fisher during Holy Week on Iona in 2007, in which he spoke of how Jesus' actions 'clarified' the image of God. This was a lens which then brought the Passion Week gospel texts into focus for me in a different way.

Encounter

Once I held you in my womb,
God sustained by woman's grace;
now the grave will close on you,
hold you in another place.

Once I nursed you at my breast,
looked with love into your face;
now your gaze is turned from me
set towards another place.

Once I travelled at your side
to the temple's holy space;
now you journey on alone
going to another place.

Though our lives seem torn apart,
still one purpose both embrace:
you through nails and I through tears
as we go towards God's place.

Text: © Pat Bennett
Tune: 'Another place'
Melody copyright © 2021 Pat Bennett
Arrangement John L. Bell, copyright © 2021 WGRG, Iona Community, Glasgow, Scotland www.wildgoose.scot

This piece was originally written for the Stations of the Cross on Iona. It is best used as a solo piece.

The last journey

Behold the Man! Betrayed, condemned, paraded;
stripped to the skin, humanity degraded;
spit on his cheeks and mocking crown set on his head –
sent on his way to death.

Crowds press and hound him, hostile faces staring;
baying and shouting, angry voices blaring;
tears of his mother, gentle hands wipe sweat away –
these the last gifts of love.

Sinews unstringing, weight of wood o'erpowering;
groans of Creation, sky above him louring;
fallen and sprawling, feeling dust beneath his cheek –
kissed by the earth he made.

Tongue parched and swollen, hands nailed down and burning,
yet still responds to love's impelling yearning:
'Father, forgive them'; 'You'll be there with me today' –
offers strong words of grace.

Darkness and doubting – 'Why do you not hear me?'
Heart's frantic anguish – 'Why with absence sear me?'
Last laboured breaths and then 'It is all finished' –
lets go his hold on life.

As Love lies vanquished, hearts and dreams are shattered;
those who believed him, frightened now and scattered;
tomb takes his body, boulder locks the light away –
hope is extinguished.

Text: © Pat Bennett
Tune: 'Iste confessor' (Poitiers Antiphoner, 1746, 11 11 11 5)

A hymn for Good Friday which could be sung as a solo or as a congregational piece (perhaps with verse 1 as a solo).

Easter story

In a garden,
surrounded by darkness,
a man kneels, abandoned and alone:
'Father, take this cup for I cannot drink it –
yet make my will one with your own.'

On a cross,
surrounded by violence,
a man hangs broken and abused:
'Father, forgive them, they don't know what they're doing.
It is finished – take my spirit back to you.'

In a tomb,
surrounded by silence,
a man rests waiting and contained:
'Even if you should destroy this temple –
in three days I will raise it again.'

In a garden,
surrounded by sunlight,
a man stands vibrantly alive:
'Go and tell my friends that I have risen
and God's Kingdom of hope has arrived.'

Text: © Pat Bennett
Tune: 'Kvällen stundar', Swedish folk tune (adapted)

This hymn is particularly suitable for an Easter Saturday vigil or an Easter Sunday dawn service. It works best as a solo piece and ideally needs two voices, one for the narrative and one for the speech of Jesus. The tune is a variation on the Swedish folk song 'Kvällen stundar'. It should not be taken too quickly, or sung in too strict a time – sing it intuitively from the text. (My apologies to any Swedish folk aficionados for my liberties here – I learnt the tune by ear from a Swedish volunteer on Iona many years ago!)

72 The Leavening of Life

Christ is here!

Feel earth's insistent song:
Hallelujah! Night is done!
Joy rumbles deep and strong:
Hallelujah! Day has come!
Dawn's fingers bless the sky,
Creation lifts the cry:
'Life lives – it will not die!'
Hallelujah! Christ is here!

Come running to the tomb:
Hallelujah! Night is done!
See sunlight shred its gloom:
Hallelujah! Day has come!
Touch where the body lay,
hear what the angels say:
'Follow him on the Way!'
Hallelujah! Christ is here!

Go spread the joyful word:
Hallelujah! Night is done!
Tell all you've seen and heard:
Hallelujah! Day has come!
Lift hearts and voices high,
send out the joyful cry:
'Love lives – it cannot die!'
Hallelujah! Christ is here!

Text: © Pat Bennett
Tune: 'Madrid' (adapted by Stephen Fischbacher ©)

This was written for the 2015 Easter Evening service in Iona Abbey. Once again these words work particularly well with Fischy Music's variation of 'Madrid'. And yes, we danced between the verses in this one as well!

Lord of Life and Resurrection

For Ellie

Lord of Life and Resurrection,
in a graveyard damp with dew,
you bequeathed God's plan and pattern
to a weak and frightened few.
And the message of their story
still today remains the same:
Lives surrendered to God's purpose
open up his Kingdom's reign!

So I set my life before you –
all its passion, joy and pain,
contradictions, strength and weakness –
to receive your touch again.
Breathe your Spirit through its textures,
shape its patterns, mend its wrong –
so my dying and my living
may release your Kingdom's song.

Take my feet and lead them outward
from the safety I would choose,
to those hard and unknown places
where you want to bring Good News.
Take my hands and through their actions
fight injustice, bring release –
by their making and their mending
show your Kingdom's hope and peace.

Take my heart and pierce its armour
that true loving may be born,
and my life become a shelter
for those weary, hurt and worn.
Take my mind and quicken insight,
sharpen questions, so I can –
through a growing understanding –
help unfold your Kingdom's plan.

Thus in journey and in action
may I make your presence real;
all my loving and my thinking
your true patterning reveal.
May the life which here I offer
make your Kingdom plain to see;
then what started in the graveyard
will continue on through me.

Text: © Pat Bennett
Tune: 'Joel' (87 87 D)

This was originally written for a confirmation service held on Easter Day. It works well with a number of tunes besides 'Joel': 'Beach Spring' gives a gentle folky feel; 'Bethany' (Henry Thomas Smart) a much more upbeat one.

Sources

'Bread' – first published in *Fire and Bread: Resources for Eastertide*, Ruth Burgess (Ed.), Wild Goose Publications, 2007, www.ionabooks.com

'Affirmation' – first published in *Iona Abbey Music Book*, Wild Goose Publications, 2003, www.ionabooks.com

'Yearnings' – first published in *Iona Abbey Music Book*, Wild Goose Publications, 2003, www.ionabooks.com

'In this darkness' – first published in *I Will Not Sing Alone: Songs for the Seasons of Love*, John L. Bell, 2004, www.ionabooks.com

'Easter story' – first published in *Fire and Bread: Resources for Eastertide*, Ruth Burgess (Ed.), Wild Goose Publications, 2007, www.ionabooks.com

Some of the pieces in this book were first published as Wild Goose downloads, www.ionabooks.com

Wild Goose Publications, the publishing house of the Iona Community established in the Celtic Christian tradition of Saint Columba, produces books, e-books, CDs and digital downloads on:

- holistic spirituality
- social justice
- political and peace issues
- healing
- innovative approaches to worship
- song in worship, including the work of the Wild Goose Resource Group
- material for meditation and reflection

For more information:

Wild Goose Publications
The Iona Community
Suite 9, Fairfield, 1048 Govan Road
Glasgow G51 4XS, Scotland

Tel. +44 (0)141 429 7281
e-mail: admin@ionabooks.com

or visit our website at
www.ionabooks.com
for details of all our products and online sales